What Shall We Do Next?

A CREATIVE PLAY AND STORY GUIDE FOR PARENTS, GRANDPARENTS AND CARERS OF PRESCHOOL CHILDREN

ANNA MALLETT
AND MARGARET MALLETT

authorHOUSE®

AuthorHouse™
1663 Liberty Drive
Bloomington, IN 47403
www.authorhouse.com
Phone: 1-800-839-8640

Published by AuthorHouse   11/14/2012

ISBN: 978-1-4772-3948-3 (sc)
ISBN: 978-1-4772-3949-0 (e)

About the Authors

Anna Mallett (D.Phil. Oxon) works in corporate management and is the mother of three pre-school children.

'One weekend I was on my own with Henry aged 2 and Freddie aged 1 and wondered what on earth I was going to do to interest them over the next 48 hours. There are trips to the shops, park and friends and, of course, routines like bathing and feeding but I wanted some ideas for activities to develop imagination and creativity. This book is the fruits of my quest and an attempt to share what I have learnt'.

Margaret Mallett (Ph.D. London) has been a primary school teacher and is now a writer and grandmother. She regularly reviews books for young children.

'There are some wonderful toys for young children in today's digital world and they have an important place in a young child's daily life. But our own input as story tellers, story readers and creators of interesting contexts for learning adventures in and out of doors is crucial to developing young imaginations'.

Contents

Introduction

For most people the experience of looking after pre-school children for extended periods starts when they become parents and continues when they become grandparents. Babies up to about a year respond to cuddling, smiling, music and action rhymes. Their development is helped by providing books that are as playful as toys with flaps to pull and buttons to press to make music. Exuberant and lively 1-3s and 3-5s enjoy activities which help stretch their imaginations and increase their concentration powers.

This book tries to help by suggesting some spur-of-the moment ideas, using simple items likely to be found in most households, and some others that, whether indoors or outside, may need a little forward planning. It also provides some hints on how to extend enjoyment of books, DVDs and TV programmes.

The principles behind the activities are those that nursery school and early years practitioners would be familiar with. Young children in a home setting also enjoy and benefit from provision of:

- Activities that involve plenty of action and interaction with others
- Imagination expanding contexts like role play, drawing and making things

- Stories in different media to enrich ideas and concepts as well as delight and entertain

The activities and suggestions are grouped under four chapter headings: 'Spur of the moment', 'Planned activities', 'Fun out of doors' and 'Choosing and using early books, television programmes, audio CDs and DVDs. There is a lot of overlap—for example stories and early fact books can enter into and enrich many of the activities. But these are so important, and now available in a range of media, that we felt they deserved a whole chapter. Home is not school, of course, and so the activities should be fun and not too formal. If at least some of these suggestions appeal to you and your young charges we would be delighted.

Age guidance

Children just a few months old can enjoy many of the activities in the book, particularly those in Chapter 1. The suggestions in chapter 2 and 3 often appeal to children aged 2-4 but can be adapted for slightly younger and older children. Chapter 4 section 3 has suggestions for babies under 12 months, including bath, cloth and board books. While some guidance is given, we've taken a flexible approach to recommending books and materials for different ages. So Chapter 4 recognises that children of the same age can have different interests and different levels of reading stamina.

The special value of books

While acknowledging that television programmes, ipads and digital texts are part of the experience of children today, we feel that paper books should be cherished. They develop imagination and thinking and provide a very special context for talk with parents and grandparents. And of course the best are hugely enjoyable. Is there research evidence to support the value of books for the very young? Yes indeed there is. A research team from the University of Pennsylvania found evidence that access to books at age 4 years and before helps develop that part of the brain to do with language and thought. Outings to parks and zoos and some kinds of educational toys also seemed to accelerate development. This team gave a paper setting out their findings in October 2012 at the Society for Neurosciences Annual Conference in New Orleans. In chapter 4 we suggest how a home bookshelf can be set up as soon as a baby arrives. Those wishing to keep up to date with recent research on books and reading development might find it helpful to visit The National Literacy Trust website: www.literacytrust.org.uk

Gender

It's best not to assume differences that don't exist. We have found that a lot of activities and stories are enjoyed by both girls and boys. Most children like making dens, engaging in role play and outdoor activities. Anything to do with nature and animals is likely to be popular with the under 5s. Lots of girls as well as boys like pirates and adventure. And many boys like picnics, role play round 'cafes' and 'tea parties'. But we have sometimes suggested some alternative activities to take account of possible gender-linked preferences and preoccupations. While lots of boys find inspiration in stories and role play about knights and kings, many girls love stories and drama that includes princesses, mermaids and fairies. When children are truly absorbed in their role play, and there's not too much rushing about, we know it is likely to be creative and satisfying.

Safety

All the activities here have been tried out with young children but of course it's important to create a safe environment. For example we need to ensure that any tables used are sturdy, that drawers are not in danger of coming out completely and that any small objects are not so tiny they could be swallowed.

Chapter 1

Spur of the moment activities

Most of us who look after young children have had those moments of panic when maybe it's raining outside and all the toys seem to have been played with and abandoned. The day looms ahead and we need to think of some interesting activities quickly so we have to improvise using our native wits!

Here are some suggested activities for those occasions when we have to use what is easily at hand. Yet these activities can be just as imagination stretching as the more planned ones. At around age 2 years Henry was inspired by the words 'Shall we have an adventure?' An 'adventure' involved simply looking round rooms, in cupboards and out of windows and talking about it. Children are also excited at the thought of secret places and hiding. Even very young babies love to be taken round the house and garden, particularly if you sing and talk to them.

1. Going on an adventure

Exploring and talking about each room and what people do in it

What you need

Nothing!

⭐ Steps

1. Say you are going on an adventure round the house
2. Ask the child if he or she wants to take a soft toy companion
3. Discuss what happens in each room—who uses it and what for
4. Select objects to look at; look under cushions
5. Look out of windows: what can we see in daytime/ at night time?
6. Bring adventure to a clear end by turning to another activity

Hints and tips

- This activity works particularly well with one child on a rainy day or when confined to home

- In bathrooms children can be fascinated with bottles and what they are used for (e.g. shampoo is used to wash mummy's hair)
- Children particularly enjoy supervised exploration of rooms they are not normally allowed in
- You could stop in each room and read a story or rhyme together before moving on. Rhymes like Pat-a-cake and Five Fat Sausages Sizzling in the Pan would be fun in the kitchen and ones about water, fish and ducks—One two three four five, Once I caught a Fish Alive and 'Row, row, row the boat gently down the stream' would suit the bathroom.

Enriching Books

The 'Let's pretend' possibilities for this 'adventure' are endless and books can enrich experience. Suggestions include:

Jan Omerod *Sunshine* Frances Lincoln. (The wonderfully bright palette tells of a young child's morning routines.)

Margaret Wise Brown *Goodnight Moon*. Macmillan (particularly inspirational for an after dark 'adventure'; it combines fact and fantasy, nursery rhyme characters and everyday objects).

Allan and Janet Ahlberg *Peepo!* Puffin. (Objects from a different time, like clothes horses, fascinate).

Mini Grey *Traction Man is Here* Red Fox. (With his small friend, Scrubbing Brush, Action Man patrols the house, hoisting fallen spoons to safety and squashing evil pillows).

Any nursery rhyme book that includes 'Twinkle Twinkle Little Star' to accompany looking out of a night time window. For example:

Paige Billan-Frye et al (illustrators) *My Treasury of Nursery Rhymes.* Igloo Books.

1.1 Rabbit's coming with me on this adventure.

2. Water play

Exploring the properties of water in a safe environment and developing vocabulary

What you need

Wash basin or kitchen sink or bucket and tray outside

Plastic cups of different sizes

Assorted spoons colanders and sieves

Brushes/cloths

Child friendly bubble bath (optional)

☆ Steps

1. Put newspaper on floor and bib on child
2. Gather together all the vessels
3. Place steady chair at sink or washbasin for child to stand
4. Supervise child as they fill and empty the vessels
5. Encourage language development by using words like 'big', 'small', 'cold', 'warm', 'too much,' 'more', 'clear up' etc.
6. Add bubbles if liked

7 Bring activity to a clear end by suggesting child helps clear up

Hints and tips

- Although you can limit the activity to water filled in the sink or bucket, children love to have the tap on, even if only dribbling
- Children enjoy helping and often like to wash their own bottles and cups
- The bath is the least messy place for water play but children seem to love standing at a sink.
- Once children have been introduced to the joys of water play they tend to want to do it a lot. So, from the beginning, set clear boundaries around when and where it takes place.

Water play box

Track down a big plastic container where water play things can be tidily stored.
Play things might include:
Things to squirt water with
Things to pour water—plastic tea-pot, tiny watering can, plastic cups, plastic measuring jug
Little boats to sail, colander and sieve
Little play people and animals to put in the boats and plastic fish.
Bath books

Enriching books

Penny Dann *The Orchard Book of Nursery Rhymes*. Orchard Books.

(This includes 'Row, row, row your boat', 'One, two, three, four five' and 'Five little ducks'.

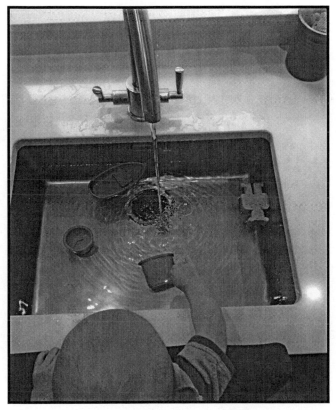

1.2. I'm after that beaker!

3. Hide and seek using soft toys

Encouraging lateral and creative thinking

What you need

Soft toy animals.

☆ Steps

1. Gather up a selection of animal toys and put them in some interesting places in the house or garden (e.g. a toy mouse in the tea-pot, a 'gruffalo' in a tree)
2. Talk to the child about the toy and where it might be hiding
3. Once found, think of a story about why the toy is there. Has another toy been unkind to it? Was it following a bee and lost its way?

Hints and tips

- The animals could be hiding in little dens
- You could ring the changes by hiding objects instead of animals—crayons, apples, a ball.

Enriching Books

Read or tell a story about a specific situation e.g. Put a mouse in a tea pot and refer to *'Alice in Wonderland'*. Helen Oxenbury's version for young children (Oxford) would be a good choice. Other books that might help include:

Nicola Smee *No Bed Without Ted* (Bloomsbury). Ted is lost and the flaps reveal where the little girl has searched;

Lauren Child *Sizzles*, a Charlie and Lola book (Bloomsbury). Sizzles is lost and the flaps show the places he might be.

4. Making a den

A game that draws on children's liking for hiding and for secret places

What you need

Toys

A stable table

Blanket or cloth

Cushion or stool

☆ Steps

1. Help child or children to put the cloth over a table or chairs.
2. Ask what they want to do in the den—play with toys, look at books, have a picnic or play 'let's pretend'
3. Help children to put in extra props to match with 2.
4. Ask them to create role play. There might be a shy teddy bear or doll that only speaks when in the den. This could lead to a dialogue. Children often like the idea of the den as a refuge from a monster or bear.

Hints and tips

- Instead of being the child or children's den, the space could be a dinosaur's cave with models of dinosaurs and pretend leaves, an animal's lair or a fairy's home
- The den can be left as part of a play area—or dismantled and re-created when needed
- Did you make dens as a child? if so children love to hear about this

Enriching Books

Read or tell a story about a den. Books include:

Shirley Hughes *Sally's Secret* (Red Fox)

Sara Gillingham & Lorena Siminovich *In My Den* (Chronicle Books)

5. Teddy and dolls' tea party

Encouraging talk and interaction in the context of role play with familiar toys

What you need

Teddies and dollies

Improvised table cloth

Plastic/paper cups

Cut up fruit/raisons

Water or weak fruit juice in a jug

☆ Steps

1. Place cloth on the floor and help child/children to set out the cups and fruit
2. Toys are chosen and are placed on the floor sitting up round the cloth
3. Food and drink is handed round
4. Tea party is brought to a clear end and children help to clear up
   (See also Chapter 3: Picnic Party)

Hints and tips

- It could be the birthday of one of the toys and Happy Birthday could be sung
- Adult can feed in interest and drama—one toy could be late or greedy
- Tea parties can include friends as part of a play day
- Tell the children about your parties when you were little

Enriching books

Sarah Garland *Coming to Tea* Frances Lincoln

Roger Hargreaves *Little Miss Tiny's Tea Party* Egmont Books

Helen Oxenbury *It's My Birthday* Candlewick Press

6. Kitchen music

Making sounds and rhythms with everyday items

What you need

Pots and pans and lids

Percussion instruments: drums, bells, rattles and tambourines

Nursery rhyme CD

☆ Steps

1. Help child to assemble the 'instruments' preferably a range of things that make different noises
2. Encourage trying out each item
3. Suggest banging quietly and then loudly
4. Talk about the sounds—high, low, loud, quiet.
5. Sing nursery rhymes for child to accompany or put on a nursery rhyme CD

Hints and tips

- This activity is particularly suitable at the younger end of the pre-school age range

- At a few months old just the chance to use some things to make a noise is enough; the other steps can be added later
- Play a nursery rhyme CD or other music to encourage rhythmic use of the percussion instruments. There are many book and CD packages with all the favourites including:
  Nursery Rhyme Book and CD Priddy Books
  Sally Gardner *Playtime Rhymes: All Our Favourites.* Orion.

1.6. Let's make a noise!'

7. In the cafe

Encourages imaginative role play with many possibilities for interesting story lines

What you need

A small table and chairs or part of kitchen table

A tea towel or similar to serve as a cloth

A tray

Cutlery

Plastic cups and plates

Small food items—pieces of fruit

Improvised menu and bill

Water or diluted fruit juice (in a jug)

Apron, coats, plastic flowers (optional)

☆ Steps

1. Ask the child or children to help set the table
2. Say you are the waiter/waitress and they are the customer/customers
3. Greet them and take their coats and give them the menu
4. Bring the items to the table, pour the drinks, ask if everything is satisfactory
5. Bring the bill
6. Bring the drama to an end by giving them their coats and waving goodbye

Hints and tips

*   Change roles—you be the customer and the child or children the waiting staff
*   Changes can be wrung by not having something available that is on the menu; keeping the customers waiting too long for their meal; getting the order wrong; dealing with a dog that has run into the cafe; pretending that a customer has left their money at home
*   Three to four year olds can be helped to write menus with pictures and to prepare bills
*   Paper money can be used
*   It's worth saying that this role playing context has been one of the most successful we have tried. Again and again children ask 'can we do the cafe play?' The secret of success seems to be to do with the many variations children themselves can make to the unfolding story. The idea of the

lost dog running into the cafe seems to have particular appeal

Enriching stories

Judith Kerr *The Tiger That Came to Tea* HarperCollins

Sarah Garland *Coming to Tea* Frances Lincoln

Chapter 2

Planned activities

These activities need not involve elaborate preparation, but having some things ready to do help make sure each day is interesting. The following suggestions work with one child or more and may be assembled while children are having a nap. They include tracking down a box and items for a miniature world and gathering objects for a secret drawer.

Once you have created the foundations for these activities they can all be used again and again and added to over time. For example a dressing—up box can be built on and last until children are at least 10 years.

1. Secret drawer

Exploiting the imaginative appeal of 'special' objects encourages conversation and questions

What you need

Cleared drawer or box

Lining paper

Objects of interest

Small treat

☆ **Steps**

1. Clear out a drawer (within a child's reach) or a box
2. Line with colourful paper
3. Choose some things the child is not normally allowed to play with (e.g. bone china figurines; sparkling jewellery; model vehicle; fancy hat)
4. Add a new item (taking out one the child is bored with) every so often
5. Make it clear that the items always stay in the drawer and are only handled with an adult there to help.

Hints and tips

- This works well with a child that visits your home—a grandchild, niece or nephew perhaps
- The drawer can contain items like birthday presents, chocolate etc as appropriate
- Things relating to family members or family history add interest for example a lace hanky, a book mummy or daddy had as children; a box carved by a grandfather or an interesting family photograph
- Or gather objects related to each other e.g. all frogs or all boxes

2.1. **Who put Rabbit in here?**

2. Pirate's treasure

Enjoying dressing up, role playing and making exciting items for the treasure box

What you need

A picture or book about pirates

A box—shoebox size

Art and craft materials: paints, scissors, glue, paper, felt and elastic to make eye patch.

The setting can be indoors, in the garden or on the beach.

☆ Steps

1. Assemble all the materials needed, including the shoe box which could be covered in silver foil and lined with material like velvet or silk
2. Show pirate picture or book or tell a pirate story (see Pirate Play at the end of this entry).
3. Explain about Pirate treasure and help children make or find items for the box: rings made out of cardboard and the stone coloured red for ruby, blue for sapphire etc.; wrap some small stones from the garden in either silver or gold paper; add

some coins—made of cardboard or chocolate coins in foil; ask children what they would like to put in—shells, small ornaments etc.

4. One person hides the box in house or garden and others find it and make a little play. With younger children you may want to limit the search to one room or one part of the garden.

Hints and tips

- Make a pirate ship with an upturned table, a sheet and a pirate flag on the top
- Black jeans/trousers and a white shirt or blouse and small, brightly coloured scarves and eye patches with felt and elastic would help develop the role play
- A beach holiday or visit is a good context for pirate activities
- Children seem ready for this activity at age two+

Enriching Books

Peter Harris and Deborah Allwright (illustrator) *The Night Pirates* Egmont Books (Some jolly girl pirates take the lead in finding the treasure, 18 months+).

Richard Walker and Olwyn Whelan (illustrator) *The Barefoot Book of Pirates* Barefoot Books (delightfully fierce pirates to stir the imagination, 2+)

Kim, Kennedy and Doug Kennedy (illustrator) *Pirate Pete.* Harry N. Abrams ('Where there's gold I'm going' says greedy Pirate Pete—vivid pictures and exciting story line, 3+).

Ronda Armitage and Holly Swain *A Home for a Pirate* Puffin (What happens if you are a pirate and you get sick of the sea? Jed finds some animals to help him find a new life—on land! 3-5 years).

Margaret Mahy and Margaret Chamberlain (illustrator) *The Man Whose Mother was a Pirate.* Puffin Picture Story Book (a lyrical pirate book—'The drift and the dreams of it . . . the fume and the foam of it never left him again' (for age 4-5 years)

A Pirate Play

Here is a basic script which could be a starting point for acting out a play. Use and change it in any way you like. Older children could make their own improvisation once given the bare bones of the simple tale. And they could be asked what they think John and Jill did with the treasure box when they got home.

Props: an upturned table with a cloth tied on to make a sail; a pretend telescope perhaps made with the cardboard middle of a kitchen roll; treasure box

Costumes: dark trousers, white shirt/blouse, coloured scarves, pirate hat.

Characters: John and Jill, an adventurous brother and sister.

John. (scanning sea from the boat) We've been on this boat a long time without seeing any land. But I think I can see an island not far away. Have a look through this telescope, Jill.

Jill. Yes, I can see yellow sand and palm trees. I'll bring our boat in to land.

(They step off the boat, tie it to a rock)

John This sand feels hot. Look there are the palm trees we could see from the boat.

(The children sit down and sip some water from the bottles they have brought).

John. What's that sticking out of the sand over there? It looks like a metal or wood object.

(The children walk over to investigate)

Jill. (scraping away the sand) It's a box. Yes—a metal box. I wonder if it is locked!

John. (forcing the lid of the box). It's treasure—look at this necklace . . .

Jill And look at those coins and rings with jewels.

John. This must be a pirate's treasure box.

(The children look at the items in the box and talk about them).

Jill. Time to get back on our boat—and we'll take the box with us

(The children return to their boat and sail away).

Discussion: What do you think happened next?

2.2. Do you like my pirate hat?

3. Dressing-up box

Building a resource for role play and improvisation

What you need

Large box or drawer

Starter items (crown, wand, sword and cloak, dark trousers, frilly skirt)

☆ Steps

1. Start using simple props like a crown, wand or vessel when reading a story e.g. use wand in a telling or reading of Cinderella and a pail to act out Jack and Jill.
2. Encourage child to dress up using props and clothes to enhance role-play
3. Act out short drama scenes together (using soft toys and dolls etc)
4. Include music—making items.

Hints and tips

- The box could be covered in bright paper or pictures

- Encourage child / children to suggest additional items for the box
- Older children might like to perform plays or stories for others
- Insist on items being tidily returned to box when role play ends
- Read picturebooks, legends and fairy tales. See also suggestions in the 'Let's Pretend' section, 2.6.
- Encourage children to make up their own stories to act out.
- Sometimes you might need to help as narrator to move the drama on.

'The most used item in our dressing up box was a large piece of muslin which served as a cloak, a head dress, a skirt, an apron or a table cloth' (Teacher and grandmother of four).

Play box for the very young

Our babies found this great fun. This is particularly helpful where there is a baby and other pre-school children in the family. While the older ones act out their plays in simple costume, the baby can be given a plastic box with some of the following items to explore and play with:

Bits of textured cloth—silk, velvet, chiffon etc.

Things that make a noise—rattles, bells, pan lids, wooden spoons to hit with

Cloth books, lift the flap books, and books with textured illustrations like those in Fiona Watts' 'That's not my . . .' series

Simple hats and scarves the baby can try on

2.3. What's in here? Hats, cloaks, wands and wings—such fine role playing things.

4. Miniature worlds: seaside scene

Helping children experience control over a small environment and practice manipulating small objects. Above all it is a starting point for talk and an impetus to storytelling and exploring ideas

<u>What you need</u>

Old tray or plastic box lid lined with blue paper for the sea and yellow paper for the sand; flat dish for 'rock pool'

Sand to sprinke over yellow paper

Toy boats

Sticky tape, card, crayons, play dough, scissors

☆ Steps

1. This activity can be based outside in the garden, on the beach or in a play area with newspaper on the floor
2. Ask child what they think is needed and have ready the sand, 'rock pool' and other items. The beach offers the stones, shells and seaweed children love to collect and use. However, they often have their own imaginative ideas for things like

improvised seaweed (grass) and can help draw, colour and cut out cardboard crabs and little fish

3. To add drama and opportunities for storytelling have available toy ambulances and rescue vehicles.

Hints and tips

- Miniature worlds are part of early years and nursery school good practice but less elaborate play with small items is enjoyed by children as young as 12-14 months.
- Finger puppets and small items round a theme or story are available commercially from The Puppet Company and Child's Play. These might provide a starting point, but selecting their own items from what is indoors or out of doors is more imagination—stretching for children and more conducive to the child feeling in charge.
- Best not to have static 'worlds' but ones with potential for action—for example predatory creatures approaching the dinosaur den or an ambulance on the beach.
- Other ideas for little worlds include: Dinosaur's den (leaves, twigs and miniature dinosaur models); Story inspired scene based on a favourite story (for example Peter Rabbit or The Gruffalo); TV inspired (for example based on The Night Garden or Thomas the Tank Engine); Dolls' house (either using a bought one or improvising with a cardboard box); Toy shop (using a tray or box for small toys). Have a car outside to transport the

toys; Garage with small vehicles and improvised petrol pumps and office

'Many children reach a stage where they are fascinated by prehistoric animals, especially dinosaurs. I cover an old tray with wrapping or tissue paper to suggest sea, beach and grassy landscape. Children can add dinosaurs and make up stories. A good idea to have some dinosaur books handy to inspire' (Grandmother of 5).

5. Making gingerbread people and animals

Introducing cooking in a way that captures the imagination

What you need

Biscuit mix

Mixing bowl, wooden spin, baking tray

Icing sugar for bow tie or ribbon, currants (for eyes and buttons) and a shred of carrot (for mouth).

☆ **Steps**

1. Make the ginger biscuit mix with flour, butter, sugar and milk (see recipe)
2. Let child stir the mix
3. Let child see you use a cutter or shape the biscuit mix into gingerbread people (or animals) and place on baking tray
4. Help child to place currant buttons and eyes and a shred of carrot for the mouth
5. Bake in oven
6. Read 'The Gingerbread Man' while the biscuits cook

There are lots of versions including:
The Gingerbread Man Ladybird Books
Estelle Corke *The Gingerbread Man: Flip flop Fairy Tales* Child's Play,
Stories for Little Boys Usborne

7. When biscuits are cool, start decorating: show child how to make a bow or ribbon with icing sugar

Hints and tips

- Children have to be allowed to make a mess during their first cooking adventures
- Best to do this when bath time is near
- Let children see you put the biscuits on a plate ready to show people; part of the satisfaction comes from arranging the food and offering others a taste

Enriching Book for cooking with children

Angela Wilkes' *Children's Step-by-Step Cookbook* Dorling Kindersley (has clear photographs showing the making and cooking stages).

Becky Johnson's *Baking with Tiny Tots: Over 50 Easy Recipes That You and Your Child Can Make* Hamlyn.

Mini Grey *Biscuit Bear* Red Fox. (Horace makes a bear with a lump of pastry. And, yes, pre-schoolers can cope with some sad realities like the fate of Biscuit Bear's friend)

There are many gingerbread biscuit recipes in print cooking books and on the Internet. Below is an eggless version we use when just making two or three gingerbread people.

Ginger biscuit mix

Ingredients

2 oz butter or margarine, softened
1 oz sugar
3 ozs flour
Pinch of cinnamon
Teaspoonful of ground ginger
Tablespoon of milk

Preparation

* Mix sugar and softened fat in a bowl until creamy
* Mix the flour, ginger and cinnamon and add it to the mixture, mixing it well
* Roll out the biscuit mix and use a shaped cutter to make gingerbread people or shape your own

* Put the biscuits on a greased baking tray and cook at Gas Mark 4, Fan oven 160 for about 10 minutes

2.5. 'Run, run as fast as you can.'

6. Let's pretend: role play and improvisation

Developing imagination and confidence

What you need

Some props and costumes to support the story or drama theme

☆ Steps

1. Discuss a favourite story with the child and ask if they would like to act it out with you
2. Ask the child which character they would like to be (for example the Gruffalo or a monster; a knight or a princess)
3. Narrate a simplified version of the story and encourage the child to participate and develop the story
4. Use different parts of the space available to enhance the story (for example the sofa could be a safe haven).
5. Change characters and add details.
   See also Chapter 2:2, Pirates' Treasure and Chapter 2.3 Dressing Up Box.

Hints and tips

- As children become more confident they will enjoy performing in front of others (for example mummy or daddy when they return from work)
- Costumes and props can help inspire further imagining (see Chapter 2.3, Dressing Up Box)
- Henry 3 and Freddie 2 were inspired to make their own play by one of the tales 'In the Castle', and particularly the illustration, in *Stories for Little Boys* (Usborne) about knights and castles.
- Sometimes children revisit a significant experience through role play. After having routine injections/vaccination, Fred at age 2.6 years wanted his soft toy rabbit to visit the doctor in his role play
- Children's current preoccupations and interests can spark off absorbed role play. After a seaside holiday, Henry at age 3 was preoccupied by what would happen if a child got lost on the beach. This led to improvisation about a lost child being taken to The Lost Children tent. Henry insisted on having a notice saying 'Lost Children'—'so that Mummies and Daddies could find their little boy or girl'.
- News stories can inspire drama too. When told about a stolen puppy, a three year old role played a happy ending, using his own toy dog.

Improvised drama with adult input.

(2.6 year old Fred had been talking about his routine inoculations)

Adult as Narrator. Mr Fred has brought Rabbit to the doctor.

Adult now becomes the doctor. How can I help you Mr Fred?

Fred. Rabbit has to have his jabs so he does not get ill.

Adult. Ah yes—I have a note here that you were coming. Please roll up his sleeve while I get the injection ready. He will feel the needle but it will not last long.

Fred. Don't worry Rabbit, it will hurt a little bit but not for long.

Doctor gives the injection.

Doctor. He has been sensible. He deserves just a little bit of chocolate I think.

Fred. Here is your chocolate because you've been a brave rabbit.

Favourite stories and rhymes to act out

Under 2s

Goldilocks and The Three Bears (see, for example, the Ladybird Tales book).

Jack and Jill; Pussycat, Pussycat where have you been?; Little Miss Muffet (see a nicely illustrated version in *My Treasury of Nursery Rhymes.* Igloo Books.)

3s and over

The Tale of Peter Rabbit by Beatrix Potter, Warne. (We have found the DVD version narrated by Niamh Cusack inspires involved improvisation).

The Ugly Duckling (see First Readers series, Marks and Spencer).

The Gingerbread Man (see the book in the Lady bird tales series or Marks and Spencers' First Readers)

The Gruffalo by Julia Donaldson and Axel Scheffle, Macmillan (especially good when done out of doors).

> 'I use a shoe box as a 'theatre' to tell the story of The Gingerbread Man. A gingerbread man biscuit from a supermarket will do, and some small figures from the toy box to represent the little old people, together with animal figures from The Early Learning Centre.'
>
> (Grandmother of 4)

Suggestions for Making up Stories about Every day Experiences from about 2 years

Once you start story telling with children, they often tell their own stories sparked off by something they see. By doing this children get a sense of narrative that feeds into reading and listening.

- You are out in the park or wood. You see a hole in a tree. Who lives there? What sort of creature? Tell a day in its life. What does it eat? Who are its friends and who are its enemies?
- Or while walking home from nursery you see some feathers on the ground. What happened here? Did the bird escape or did the fox capture it?

'Freddie, aged 3, found a ladybird costume in the depths of the dressing—up box and squeezed himself into it. He began creeping under tables and chairs saying' I'm a little ladybird and I'm looking for a home'. Brother Henry, aged 4, leapt up shouting 'I'm a bird and I'm looking for an insect to eat for my dinner!' I then joined in saying I was a cat looking for a bird to devour'. (Mother of three).

Books to inspire talk and role play on a Prince/Princess theme

From about age 2 and a half years stories in books or on DVDs give a structure for children's role play. Some stories turn convention on its head so that it is the princess who fights the dragon or rides the horse or drives the motor bike. Here are some suggestions for conventional stories and stories playing with the usual pattern of events.

Conventional stories

The Usborne Book of Princess Stories. Heather Amery and S. Cartwright (illustrator). Suitable for age 2 and over.

The Princess and the Pea, Cinderella, titles in Marks and Spencers' First Readers and Ladybirds' First Readers.

Sally Gardner and Emma Chambers (reader) *A Book of Princesses* Orion (book and audio CD with five favourite stories told as fairies sew pearls on the Queen's ball gown, for about age 3 and over).

Cinderella: A Pop-up Fairy Tale. Matthew Reinhart. Simon and Schuster (a classic retelling using imaginative paper engineering and colourful illustrations for the over threes under supervision).

Stories that reverse convention

That's Not My Princess Fiona Watts Usborne.

Taps into what children think a princess should be like. One princess is 'too bumpy'. Textured illustrations work well from silky dresses to fluffy fans. Suitable from about 18 months.

Babette Cole *Princess Smartypants* Picture Puffin. Here it is the motor bike riding princess who challenges her princes.

Prince Cinders, also by Babette Cole, is about a prince who is bullied by his three hairy brothers. This is a reversal of the Cinderella story as it is the prince's fortunes that change when a fairy intervenes . . .

The Paperbag Princess by Robert Munsch and Michael Martchenco, Annick Press. This rings the changes round the usual 'princess captured by a dragon' tales. It is probably best to read it to children approaching age five who have heard the more traditional versions.

Feedback from Amazon customers suggests that younger children, and boys as well as girls, find the story entertaining. It starts in a castle and ends in a cave.

Mermaid tales to encourage storying and drama

Fiona Watt *That's Not My Mermaid* Usborne. Like the other titles in the touchy feely textured books, this one appeals to the imaginations of the very young from about 18 months onwards

Michelle Trowell & Kirsten Richards (illustrator) *Magical Mermaids* Top Hat Publishing. Rhyming text inspires children to use magnetic pieces to make underwater pictures of the mermaids at play.

Russell Punter, Lesley Sims & Desideria Guicciardin *Stories of Mermaids* Usborne. There are speech bubbles and lovely illustrations in a book particularly liked by girls from about age 3 and a half; good for shared reading or for older children to read on their own.

Fairy Stories to encourage talk and improvisation

Fiona Watts *That's Not My Fairy* Usborne. The shiny textured illustrations by Rachel Wells work extremely well in this book from the well liked touchy feely series. Children enjoy it from about 18 months to two and a half and love joining in the repeated line: 'That's not my fairy . . .'

Jane Ray *The Dolls' House Fairy* Orchard. In this beautiful picturebook, Rosy discovers a fairy called Thistle who lives in her dolls' house. Enjoyable from about age 3 upwards.

Lorna Read and Jan Lewis (illustrator) *The Elves and the Shoemaker. First Favourite Tales.* Ladybird. This is one of the titles in Ladybird's series of retellings of classic fairy tales. This one is about a poor shoemaker who wakes up one morning to find that elves have made shoes for his customers. Rhythm, rhyme and lively illustrations combine to make this enjoyable for children from about age 2 upwards.

Ladybird Tales. There are 24 in the series including *Cinderella* and *Goldilocks and the Three Bears.*

Lauren Child *My Completely Best Story Collection.* Puffin. This Charlie and Lola audiobook adopts an original take on the traditional fairy tale and includes a story about The Tooth Fairy. Enjoyed from about 18 months upwards.

'After seeing a play based on Shaun the Sheep, two year old Rafael got th idea of coming out from behind curtains to recite and sing songs' Mother of 1.

2.6 a.'Have some tea and a slice of cake.

2.6b. I'm a fierce monster!

7. Rituals

Reinforcing family traditions at home or helping make visits to relatives interesting and fun. Some of the ideas already covered in this book, including 'Going on an adventure' and 'Secret drawer', may become rituals. Here we set out two further examples and some 'Hints and Tips'

Suggestion 1: Tea Making

What you need

Child's tea set; Granny's favourite cup and saucer

☆ Steps

1. This is a good activity during a visit to granny and grandfather—have everything ready for the child's arrival
2. Preparations will probably include getting out the children's tea-set (and, yes, little boys like this as much as do girls) and Granny's favourite teapot, cup and saucer and ingredients for making the tea. Milk and /or lemon slices can be laid out ready.
3. Child can watch Granny make her tea; using a tea strainer adds interest.

4. Then a little mouthful of weak, milky tea can be put in the child's tea-pot to pour under supervision
5. Consider reading or telling Beatrix Potter's *Tale of Peter Rabbit* (Warne) in which Peter is given some camomile tea to sooth him after a terrifying adventure in Mr McGregor's Garden.

Young children make connections between literature and life in interesting ways.

'After hearing The Tale of Peter Rabbit read by Granny, my 3 year old suggested that the nursery teacher give an upset child "some camomile tea to calm her" '

Suggestion 2: Cooking together

What you need
Cooking utensils and ingredients

☆ Steps

1. Children love to cook with a relative and it becomes an eagerly anticipated part of the visit
2. Although the emphasis should be on enjoyment, many words and concepts can be learnt in this context: measuring, stirring, tasting and decorating

3. Best not to allow clambering on chairs to reach things. Children can use a safety set of steps or ask to be lifted up
4. This is a good opportunity to supervise children using cooking tools and electric appliances safely
5. When the cooking is complete and everything tidied away, the child can be asked what they would like to make on the next visit; it's good to give choices and the child can start anticipating the next occasion

Enriching Books

There are lots of cookery books for the very young to share.

Angela Wilkes' *Children's Step-by-Step Cookbook* (Dorling Kindersley) has clear photographs showing the making and cooking stages and which has savoury as well as sweet items

Becky Johnson's *Baking with Tiny Tots: Over 50 Easy Recipes That You and Your Child Can Make* (Hamlyn).

Hints and tips

- Shared activities may arise from an adult's hobby-gardening, sewing, caring for pets or art and craft.

- Make a scrap book of activities. It could include photographs of your child making tea or cooking with granny together with some recipes. Some of the recipes could be from other members of the family and headed 'Auntie Katherine's Scrumptious Cracklets' or 'Grandfather's Savoury Cheese Toast'
- Gardening enthusiasts often let their grandchild nurture a small garden and watch the lettuce, mint and carrots grow. Gardening is seasonal and here again a book of photographs and drawings would be something to share with others
- Children often love talking about family history and regard this as part of a visit to grandparents. Old photographs, medals, fossils, trophies, china, clothing, jewellery or hand made things keep family history alive and start off reminiscences about when Granny or Grandfather were little
- Seasonal rituals may include painting Easter eggs with Grandfather, Christmas shopping with granny and decorating the tree and preparations for apple bobbing at Halloween

Chapter 3

fun out of doors

Computers, multi-channel television and computerised toys using the latest technology are very much part of children's early experience of the world. Nothing wrong with this. But too much exposure to all this secondary and virtual experience, at too young an age, may risk making children less creative in their play and exploration of the world. Therefore there is all the more reason to give children opportunities to experience the life-enhancing joys of outdoor environments.

The following suggestions are built round such simple things as exploring the family garden and also the wild environment of the beach, park and wood. Then there is the urban out of doors—train stations, art galleries and museums.

All this is likely to put children's creativity and their imaginations into top gear. Not only will these experiences help them develop a multitude of technical and social skills they will also gain a sense of the satisfactions interacting with real things brings.

1. Painting activities outside

Gives freedom to paint on a large scale, using face, body and paper

What you need

A sunny day!

Large pieces of paper and non toxic finger paint

'Clothes line' display area

Flannels and old towels

A mirror and a camera

Chair or stool

☆ **Steps**

1. Find a shady place in the garden and set out paints and a selection of different sizes of paper
2. Have a wash and brush up area with damp flannels and old towels
3. Set up a display area for children to look at each other's pictures

4. Set up a face and body painting area with chair, camera and a mirror so that children can look at their faces
5. Bring activities to an end by looking at each other's faces and pictures and taking some photographs
6. Finally—a grand clean-up

Hints and tips

- Best out of doors on a warm day, but can be done in an indoor play area
- Can be done with one child, but more fun with some friends from age 2-3 years
- Bring activity to an end when children stop concentrating, and show the display of paintings
- Before or after the activity read *Cave Baby* by Julia Donaldson and Emily Gravett (Puffin). Cave baby meets a hare, a tiger and a hyena and after a wonderful ride on a hairy mammoth's back, scribbles some cave paintings.
- A book which will appeal to some young artists is Eric Carle's 'Draw Me a Star' (Puffin).

2. Nature observation walks

Helps increase sensory awareness in a way suitable at all times of the year and adaptable for different ages

What you need

Bag to collect specimens

Magnifying glass

Sketchbook, paints and crayons

Camera

☆ **Steps**

- 2-3 year olds will be able to help plan the walk
- Make a simple map of the route to the park, wood or outdoor space, asking the child or children what they might see (for example, squirrels in the trees)
- Get the specimen bag, sketchbook and magnifying glass ready and ask the children how they could use them
- If you have a camera to take, ask children how this could be helpful (to make a record of creatures spotted like birds and squirrels)

- When you reach the park or wood encourage them to look for tiny things like beetles and spiders as well the big things like trees and bushes
- Encourage them to use noses and ears as well as eyes
- Share the finds—leaves, stones etc once home and either display them on a table or make a scrap book to which photographs can be added later
- Show children how to draw round leaves and then paint within the shape

Hints and tips

- Explain that leaves and stones are fine to bring back, but living creatures like spiders and snails are best left in their habitat
- This is a golden opportunity to introduce children to non-fiction books, but the emphasis should be on enjoyment. Some children are interested in identifying plants and creatures from an early age, others might be put off by too 'schoolish' an approach
- Three nature books which suggest where to look are Steve and Charlotte Voake's *Insect Detective* (Walker Books Nature Storybook), Christina Goodings' *Out and About in My Boots* (Lion Children's Books) and Mick Manning and Brita Granstrom's *Nature Adventures* (Frances Lincoln).

3.2.This is my friend with a beautiful pattern on his shell.

3. Going to the shops

Helping children feel included in every day activities; learning about colour, quantity and the concept of money

What you need

Shopping list

☆ Steps

1. Write a list of things you need from the shops, including the child and discussing which shops you need to visit
2. Within the shop look at displays and items of interest noting colours (let's look for red fruit), shapes (that cheese is in the shape of a triangle) and numbers (how many bottles of shampoo are on that shelf?)
3. Ask the child to help in the selection of items—locating them and helping to decide what should be purchased
4. When it comes to paying, count out the money with the child or explain the credit card
5. Ask the child to help put things away when you get home

Hints and tips

- Perhaps the child could choose a small item (e.g. a child's magazine) and pay the shop keeper directly themselves
- Very young children will enjoy sitting in the trolley and handling some of the items (e.g. packets)

Enriching books

Sarah Garland *Going Shopping* Frances Lincoln. Mum, toddler, baby and dog all go by car to the supermarket. The detail in the illustrations and the different families shown are excellent talking points

Max Harvey *Shopping with Dad* Barefoot Books. An entertaining story in rhyme showing how this family copes with some entertaining mishaps on a shopping trip. Shows the different people out shopping.

Stella Blackstone and Christopher Corr *My Granny went to market* Barefoot Books. Nothing as boring as food shopping here! Granny buys fascinating things in different countries. The wonderfully vibrant pictures and energetic story line will appeal to toddlers.

4. Picnic party with teddies and soft toys

Gives scope for role play and social interaction in a jolly out of doors context

What you need

Coloured card and crayons for invitation

Cloth or rug

Picnic basket

Plastic tea-set

Party food

 Steps

1. Make simple invitations for friends using coloured card and crayons
2. Ask invitees to bring a favourite soft toy or doll
3. On the day, get children over about 2 years to prepare the sort of things bears like (sandwiches and fruit)
4. Let child or children help to set out a cloth in the garden or park
5. Set out the food and drink (keeping further supplies in picnic basket)

6. Welcome arriving guests and admire their toys; children show their toy and tell the others its name
7. Play some party games—pass the parcel, ring a roses
8. Songs and stories while adults clear up e.g *Teddy Bears Picnic: Nursery Rhymes, Stories and Songs*, ASIN BOOK X 21PDA.
    See also Chapter 1:5 'Tea party with Teddies and Dolls.

Hints and tips

- Make sure children feel their special toy has been appreciated
- Out of doors is the place to sing 'The Teddy Bears' Picnic' (If you go down to the woods today . . .)
- Adult could tell a story about a picnic while others clear up
- Or read a story, for example:
  'This is the Bear and the Picnic Lunch' by Sarah Hayes (Walker Books)
  Having a Picnic by Sarah Garland (Frances Lincoln)
  'We're going on a picnic' Pat Hughes (Red Fox)
  Piglet's Picnic Jessica Souhami Frances Lincoln
  Spot's First Picnic and Other Stories Eric Hall Grosset Dunlop.
- Children coming up to three would enjoy acting out a picnic story, perhaps with adult as narrator
- If it is a birthday picnic, simple party bags would please, with teddy bear stickers and balloons

Bare bones of a picnic story

Children could volunteer in turn to act out a picnic story in twos and threes. In our experience, the other children make an enthusiastic audience.

Narrator. Once upon a time some children (say their names) were having a picnic with their mother, big sister, aunt or granny.

(Children supply some conversation).

Narrator. The children slipped away to explore the wood and find some interesting things—a snail, ladybird, wild flowers etc. Children decide what to include here.

(Children supply conversation)

Narrator. Then they see something moving behind a tree.

(Children talk about what it could be. A gruffalo or bear perhaps!)

Narrator They thought they should go back to Mummy quickly. Mummy said they should not have wandered off on their own. The children told their mother about seeing the tail of a strange creature. Just then there was a meow sound and a large tabby cat walked past!

The mystery of the monster in the woods was solved!

5. In the garden or park

Using open air spaces available all the year round for exploring and learning.

The Garden.

Those lucky enough to have even a small back garden have a handy, healthy, readymade bit of countryside. As you have control over your garden you can make it a clean and exciting area for children to play.

Activities

* Sand and water play: make a sand tray and collect together buckets, spades, pouring vessels like colanders, old tea pots and plastic jugs and bottles and allow the child to experiment. Provide a plastic bucket of water.
* Studying animals and plants: find an ant or leaf and look at it close up. Use a magnifying glass to see the details. Talk about colour and shape.
* By age 3 years children enjoy having their own little garden and planting seeds and making a pattern with stones. For inspiration track down Eddie's Garden by Sarah Garland (Frances Lincoln)
* For other activities in the garden see chapter 3.1 (Painting outside), Chapter 3.3 (Nature Walks) and Chapter 3.4 (Picnics)

I'm fascinated by the veins and colours
on this leaf.

Garden Box

Seek out a large plastic container or bucket to store items, for example:

Watering can

Spades and trowels of different sizes

Transparent collection box to observe mini beasts before putting them back where they were found

Sticks

Plastic bowls to make 'ponds'

Plastic animals, vehicles and play people to make little scenes on the grass

Children's tea-pot and plastic cups and a tea towel to serve as a cloth for a teddies' picnic

The Park

A trip to the park can offer the opportunity to expend a lot of energy! Here are some of the things you can do beyond visiting the playground, swings and sandpit.

Activities

* Extend the study of animals and plants begun in the garden (see Chapter 3.2 Nature Observation Walk).
* Play 'Hunt the Gruffalo'. Adult pretends to be a gruffalo or other friendly monster and chases the children. A 'safe' den can be agreed where the children can escape and hide.
* Other ideas for out of doors drama include:
  The Teddy Bear's Picnic (see Chapter 3.4 'Picnic Party); The Lost Doll, Teddy or Dog; The Wounded Bird, Rabbit or Kitten.

Enriching Books

Steve Voake and Charlotte Voake (illustrator) *Insect Detective* Walker Books (has wonderfully detailed pictures of the creatures to help with identification) 2+.

Sarah Garland *Eddie's Garden and how to make things grow*. Frances Lincoln (full of information to answer children's questions—set in the context of an appealing story about a young child's activities out of doors) 2+

Vivian French and Jessica Ahlberg *Yucky Worms* Walker (a good story and excellent cross sections of the worms underground)3+

Steve Smallman and Jack Tickle *The Very Greedy Bee* Little Tiger Press (What happens when Greedy Bee will not share his nectar?) 3+

Jack Tickle *The Very Busy Bee* Little Tiger Press (has exciting illustrations e.g. of ants and snails close up but, as with all delicate pop-ups, needs to be used under supervision)2+

Mick Manning and Brita Granstrom *Nature Adventures* Frances Lincoln (3 to 5s and above can learn from the interesting text and the vignettes of plants and animals).

3.5 a. I'm fascinated by the veins and colours on this leaf.

3.5 b. I'm helping.

6. On the beach

Provides endless space and resources for learning and play in a distinctive and rich environment

What you need

Buckets

Spades and other implements to dig and make patterns and draw in the sand

A transparent plastic bowl to store creatures that need water

Containers for finds

Small items: little flags to put on castles, small figures to enhance sand pictures and a little bag containing pretend coins and jewels for pirate's treasure

Activities

- Counting-waves, shells and pebbles
- Collecting shells, sticks, stones and seaweed to create sand gardens and pictures
- Collecting creatures like tiny crabs and fish that should be soon returned to rock pools
- Building shapes in the sand and decorating them
- Sorting shells by size and colour

- Making a mini rock pool in see-through bowl using different kinds of sea weed
- Drawing pictures in the sand

Hints and tips

- See also Pirate's Treasure (Chapter 2.2) and Miniature Worlds (Chapter 2.4)
- Drama round the theme of The Lost Child, The Lost Puppy or The Lost Teddy (see also Let's pretend, 2.6)

Enriching books

These can be read before or during the visit or enjoyed afterwards to resavour the experiences

Jill Bennett and Nick Sharratt *Seaside Poems* Oxford University Press (pictures and poems about different times of year on the beach)3+

Margaret Wise Brown and Anne Mortimer (illustrator) *Sneakers, the Seaside Cat* (visiting the seaside from a cat's viewpoint) 4+

Mick Manning and Brita Granstrom *Seaside Scientist*. Franklin Watts (about spotting creatures that live on the beach, cliffs and dunes) 4+

Mick Manning and Brita Granstrom *High Tide, Low Tide* Wonderwise series, Franklin Watts (helps adult and child identify plants and sea plants). 4+

7. Urban outings: train stations, museums, galleries and zoos

Encourages confidence away from home and helps develop observation skills and social awareness.

What you need

Clothes suitable for weather and activities

Camera

A toy or game for the journey

Little bag for post cards etc

☆ Steps

1. Do any preparation that will help, checking opening times, children's activities that day, facilities and other visitor information—sounds obvious, but we have all been caught out . . .
2. Plan the day with child or children: talk about the outing; why you are going, things to take, the journey and what you will see. A relevant book on trains, museums, art galleries or zoos often focuses attention and increases anticipation

3. Talk about what you need to take—a drink, lunch perhaps, wellingtons . . .

4. Children often like to take their own small bag or rucksack for 'finds' or items from the shop

5. When the visit is over and you come home, there may be some interesting things to follow up. Tell someone else about the visit—telephone Granny perhaps. Art activities round the day prolong the experience and are something else to show others.

Hints and tips

Train stations

* Children love visiting steam railways like the Bluebell and having a ride. If your outing is to a train station, it is probably best to choose a small local station where there is ease of access and you can stand on a not too busy platform or view the trains from a bridge. Things to do include:
* Looking at changing signal colours and at the points as station gets ready for the trains coming
* Count the number of trains you see—you could write this down for the child in a notebook
* Count the number of carriages and comment on their colour
* Listen to the announcements and look at the indication board
* Talk about where the trains have come from and where they are going

Museums and galleries

If you are visiting a museum or art gallery a plan of your visit is essential. Check with the child whether they would like to see dinosaurs, armour or costumes and prepare them with a book or picture for a museum visit. If you are visiting an art gallery a preliminary visit would help. You could buy post cards of pictures you think would appeal and make tracking them down part of the excitement of the outing.

Zoo visits

These are also more likely to be successful if carefully planned and children's preferences about which animals to see are taken account of. Check things like special activities for children and animals feeding times. Don't try to see everything. Follow-up is important—drawing and painting the animals seen and telling someone about the visit, and planning what you would like to see on a follow-up visit.

Enriching boks

Fiona Watts and Rachel Wells *That's Not My Train.* Usborne Board Book. Children around age 2 years enjoy the colours and textures in this lively book.

Jemima Lumley and Sophie Fatus *Journey Ho from Granpas.* Book and CD, Barefoot Books. 'T. purple train speeds along the shiny railway track All sorts of vehicles are seen on this journey, including a train.

Jess Stockham *Down By the Station.* Child's Play. All the things you see at the station—taxis, buses, ticket office etc. This lovely book comes in board book from for babies and in paperback format for pre-school children.

Emily Bone *Trains* Usborne Beginners. Towards age four or five, some children are ready to share more demanding books with an adult. For young train enthusiasts this book covers different kinds of train—steam, diesel and electric and has clear contents page, glossary and index.

Vivian French and Alison Bartlett *T.Rex* Candlewick Press. Lovely rhyming story about a boy and his grandfather's visit to a museums dinosaur section. Lots of interesting questions and speculations.

Lucy Micklethwait *I Spy Colours* HarperCollins. There's a red key, a black cat and a yellow sun to spot.

Brian Wildsmith *Zoo Animals* Star Bright Board book. Appealing pictures and interesting facts.

Chapter 4

Choosing and using early books, television programmes, audio CDS and DVDS

Introduction

Of all the ideas in this book to fill a child's day with interesting and valuable activities, reading and talking about stories and early fact books is one of the most worthwhile. Books can be shared at any age and at any time of day. Don't wait until they can talk before you introduce them to books. Children are sociable beings from the beginning of their lives, eager to make meaning out of all they experience and to share those experiences with people they trust.

What do children get from stories? First, and most important of all, they are the perfect way to expand thinking and imagining. Young listeners are taken into different situations and environments and follow the adventures of different characters. The best storie make us want to know what will happen next. Second, stories help children to concentrate and listen and, of course, they are a brilliant way of developing language. Rhyming stories are particularly good for helping children to remember a story from one reading to the next and that is why they are so well represented in our recommendations. Not only does vocabulary increase because new words are heard in the context of a story, but children also benefit from the conversation that accompanies the reading.

Third, stories play a big part in helping children learn about their world and the values held dear in their culture. Think of the lasting impact of meeting Peter Rabbit, Mog and the Gruffalo and other countless characters in children's books for the important pre-school age group.

Fourthly, children's capacity for feeling as well as thinking develops enormously in the first few years of life. Stories help us empathise with others and to be sympathetic to how they might feel.

In recent years there has been a burgeoning of the picture book, an illustrated book where pictures and writing combine to tell a tale. So this part of the book includes suggestions for 'must haves' in this category. Other annotated lists are Rhymes to Sing and Move To, Bath, Cloth and Board Books for Babies and Stories on Television and DVD. Multimedia input is now very much part of our culture and so stories in electronic media have a place in a child's collection while we continue to cherish traditional print books. The two final listings take children into early non-fiction literature. Engaging and important as stories are, the best non-fiction for children can be original and exciting and can be introduced very early on. Two important non-fiction forms for young children are information stories which embed factual material in a narrative and concept books to help children learn about and enjoy 'abcs', and books about number, shape, comparison and colour.

While we offer advice on choosing books and resources and make some suggestions for extending response, children are individuals with their own preferences and interests. You will know about these. The first section offers some hints for parents about starting a young child's home library. The author, Anne Fine, put the idea of a home library for every child at the centre of her programme as the second Children's Laureate. We hope that the other sections in this chapter will be helpful also to grandparents, and friends of the family and indeed anyone who wishes to buy books and DVDs for under fives.

1. Hints about starting a young child' home library

a.) Start a book collection for your child. Each child in the family should have their own collection although, realistically, the children in the family will have many books in common. Having ownership of some favourite books is an excellent way of encouraging your child to enjoy and value them

b.) Clear a small shelf or cover a large box with wrapping paper

c.) Bookplates with the child's name can be placed in the books. These can be bought, you can make your own using sticky paper or you can download some for free by famous children's authors from www.myhomelibrary.org. Encourage the child to return a book to the shelf or box after it has been read.

d.) Start with short reading sessions as children's concentration spans develop over time

e.) Make links between the story and the child's recent experience. If you saw a cat when you were out, make the link with the cat in the book

f.) Keep alert with the new picturebooks that pour into bookshops by browsing free catalogues from major bookshops and look at displays of new children's books. Read reviews on websites specialising in children's books, for example

    a. Books for Keeps on—line www.booksforkeeps

    b. The Book Trust www.booktrustchildrensbooks.org.uk

Our five 'must have' picture books to start the collection

1. **Owl Babies** by Martin Waddell illustrated by Patrick Benson (Walker Board Books)

'Where is Mum?' wonder three baby owls when they wake up to find they are alone in the night time wood. Mum returns to an ecstatic welcome and all is well. At six months babies respond to the feathery end pages, by a year many love to see the creamy owlets against a darkening sky and by about two years they can begin to understand the story.

2. **The Very Hungry Caterpillar** by Eric Carle, Puffin Board Book

This classic picture book delights each new generation of children. The die-cut pages help with colours and counting, but it is most of all a wonderful story about metamorphosis

3. **Peepo!** By Janet and Peter Ahlberg, Puffin Books

The lively rhyming text and endearing illustrations have enormous appeal for young children, even though the pictures show objects from an earlier period. It's in many formats including a board book version.

4. **Dear Zoo** by Rod Campbell, Puffin Books

Now in many different formats and media, including paper and board and even a Buggy Book version, after twenty five years since first publication, this classic still fascinates and amuses young listeners. Pop-ups add appeal.

5. **Goodnight Moon** by Margaret W Brown, illustrated by Clement Hurd. Macmillan Book Board

This robust little hardback is the right size for small fingers to hold. The pictures tell of a different time—there is a coal fire and an old fashioned telephone in the green room-yet there is something universal about the nursery rhyme pictures on the wall and the night time sky with moon glimpsed through the window. Text is minimal—'Goodnight bears, goodnight chairs'—but the rhymes are remembered.

New potential classics appear all the time. Look out for:

Sam Lloyd *Whose Tail?* Little Tiger Press. 'The cheeky monkey pulls the tail of . . . 'An entertaining book enjoyed from about 10 months. This has the clear bright pictures children love.

Mini Grey *Toys in Space*, Jonathan Cape. Under fives will love this space adventure! Blue Rabbit suggests a space

…ry might cheer the toys up after they are left outside the dark . . .

Oliver Jeffers *How to Catch a Star* Philomel Books. About a boy's longing for a star of his own.

Polly Dunbar *Penguin* Walker Books. What can you do when your toy penguin does not respond? A most original and intriguing story with stunning minimalist illustrations.

David Lucas *Whale* Andersen. Distinctive and beautiful illustrations match an intriguing story.

Nicola Davies and Brita Granstrom *Dolphin Baby* Walker Books. Beautifully pictured account of a baby dolphin's first experiences in his watery world.

Ruth Brown *Ten Seeds* Andersen Press. What happens when a child plants ten seeds? Board book with excellent, and hugely appealing pictures.

Are some stories too frightening for the under fives?

Young children sometimes come across things that frighten them in books. It is difficult to know what might disturb particular children. A two year old known to us liked her nursery rhyme book but wanted to stop looking at it when the Wee Willie Winkie picture came up. Some children are alarmed by particular animals. A child within our family had a strong reaction to the

pop-up picture of a huge spider that springs out on t
last page of '*I'm Not Scary!* by Rod Campbell. He sti
asked for the book to be read but wanted it put on a
high shelf between readings, perhaps to give him some
control. *At* around age 3 years another child, Rafael, did
not like to see foxes pictured or mentioned in stories His
mother thought this seemed to arise from an incident
when a fox took away one of his father's shoes from
their front door. Frightening stories can help children
cope with their fears and to make anxieties explicit.
A certain amount of excitement can be entertaining.
Perhaps there are two things to bear in mind. First,
frightening things in stories should be overt and not
hidden and vague. Second, things should be resolved
by the end of the story.

Here are three books your young children might find
exciting without being terrifying.

Jonathan Allen *I'm Not Scared.* Boxer Board Book. Baby
owl goes into a wood at night. But being an owl—he
should not be scared . . .

Julia Donaldson *The Gruffalo* Macmillan. This is a
monster children cope with well, perhaps because of
the resourcefulness of the mouse and the rhyming text
full of humour.

Pat Hutchins *Rosie's Walk.* Red Fox. After more than
40 years in print this famous hen's walk through the
farmyard, followed by a rather dim fox, still enchants.

4.2 'I like my DVDs but I love my books too.'

Some comments by grandparents about children's books

'The Gruffalo is the book I most enjoyed sharing with my grandchildren when they were aged two or three. The rhyming text drives the story and they found it so exciting when the Gruffalo actually turns up. They really cared about the safety of the resourceful little mouse.' Grandfather of five.

'Our 2 and a half year old likes books that explore feelings—*Owl Babies* by Martin Waddell, *Ginger* by

Charlotte Voake and particularly Edward Ardizzone's book *Johnny's Bad Day.* What is in books like these seems to influence how children see the world and begin to understand the feelings of others as this conversation suggests.

Child. Ellie was cross and sad like Johnny at nursery today.

Granny. Oh dear, why was she sad?

Child. 'Cos I ate her sandwich'

(Granny of five)

3. Rhymes and stories to sing and move to

Why are these important?

Babies are active creatures who want to be 'alive in the world' from the very earliest weeks. Rhymes and songs provide a context for interaction with parents and carers and help develop social skills and language. The non-verbal element involving gestures and movement complements the language which is often rhythmic and playful. As well as nursery rhymes, there are wonderful rhyming stories for this age group.

Interactive activities children can engage in

- Say or sing the rhymes with the sharing adult. This is a chance to appreciate the charm of rhythm and rhyme, language play and humour
- Talk about all the things the characters are doing
- Join in the actions: finger play enhances enjoyment of 'Incy Wincey Spider', 'Round and Round the Garden' and 'This Little Piggy'
- Use some simple props to add to the fun of acting out the rhymes: a toy spider and a cushion for the Little Miss Muffet rhyme, a little bag or purse for Lucy Locket and a plastic pail for Jack and Jill

Some favourite books

The Orchard Book of Nursery Rhymes for Your Baby illustrated by Penny Dann, (Orchard Books) is large and colourful and appeals as soon as you pick it up because it is so generously spaced. Each chosen rhyme is beautifully set in a page with a lovely contemporary illustration. Look at the expressions on the faces of the three little kittens—in an icy landscape without their mittens. And, oh dear, Miss Muffett seems to be actually turning into a spider! The collection is nicely organised, too, with sections including 'This Little Piggy', 'All the King's Men', 'One, Two, Three, Four Five',' Work, Rest and Play' and 'Hush Little Baby'. Out of all the many nursery rhyme collections we have perused, this one stands out as ideal for the pre-school age-group.

Peek-a-boo Baby by Mandy Ross and illustrated by Kate Merrit, Ladybird Rhyming Flap Book is a book to get babies of only a few months of age responding to images in books and listening to the sharing adult's reading. Each page has a baby hidden beneath an object like a teddy bear or ball which is revealed when the flap is lifted. Opposite is a rhyme describing the picture. The last page has a mirror into which the baby can smile. Another good option is *Ring-a-ring O' Roses and Other Nursery Rhymes* illustrated by Brita Granstrom, Walker. This jolly lift-the-flap book has eight nursery rhymes which call out for young listeners to join in. The active children in the pictures encourage singing, dancing and bouncing.

The Bedtime Collection compiled by Wendy Cooling, Orchard (donation of proceeds is made to the Book trust charity) is another rich compendium. This large, collection of poems and stories introduces young children to some of the best current writers and illustrators for the pre-school years: Shirley Hughes, Quentin Blake, Michael Morpugo, Tony Ross and many others. Here older toddlers will find some less familiar rhyming stories and poems and the book contains such delights as Jez Alborough's 'Duck in a truck'—'This is the duck, who waves from the truck' and Nick Butterworth's 'Bouncing'—'Bouncing up and down, It's hard to frown'. There's also 'I love Ketchup' by Giles Andreae and Korky Paul and Benjamon Zephaniah and Jan Omerod's 'Me. Me, Me'.

Room on the Broom by Julia Donaldson and illustrated by Axel Scheffler, Campbell Books. Julia Donaldson has a rare skill with rhymes, as fans of her Gruffalo books know, This rhyming. story about the friendly, eccentric witch with her 'tall hat' and 'long ginger plait' enthrals most children of about age two years and older ones will enjoy joining in and following it up with role play and drawing.

Wheels on the Bus, Pre-school Songs, BBC Audio CD has traditional nursery rhymes and songs and some newer favourites. It includes songs that invite bouncing, dancing and singing, for example 'Row, Row, Row Your Boat', 'If you're Happy and You Know It, Clap Your Hands' and 'The Grand Old Duke of York'. Worth considering also is the sister BBC CD *Incy Wincey Spider* which has several counting rhymes.

Bath, cloth and board books for babies' first twelve months

A baby's very first books are likely to be close to toys. So we have squeaking plastic bath books, cloth books with lots of different textures to feel and robust board books that often have flaps to lift. The best ones have high contrast illustrations—black and white is a winner for example—and offer the chance for baby to interact and respond. Any good children's book department will have an exciting choice of these. Here are some suggestions:

Axel Scheffler *Freddie the Frog Bath Book.* Campbell Books. This book about Freddie and his friends is buoyant—so does not sink to the bottom of the bath. Children like the squeaker, even if this is not a frog's authentic sound!

Stella Bagott. *Baby's Very First Black and White Bath Book* Usborne. This has lovely simple pictures—of an octopus and a turtle for example.

Jo Moon *Fluttery Fish* Campbell Books. A colourful, shaped book which has a useful special sucker to attach to the side of the bath.

Jungly Tails, Little Jellycat series. This soft cloth book provides lots of entertainment for babies— they can pull the tails at the side of the book and feel the different textures. Great fun!

Stella Bagott Baby's very first touchy-feely book. Usborne. High contrast pictures make this book stand out. Lumpy crocodile, for example, is bright green with sharp white teeth against a black background.

Eric Hill _Where's Spot?_ Warne. Children coming up to their first birthday love this lift-the-flap board book. Spot is hiding from Mum. Where can he be?

Allan Ahlberg and Janet Ahlberg _The Baby's Catalogue_ Puffin. This fine board book (also in paperback) has stood the test of time. The collections of everyday objects of five different families are set out and inspire much talk.

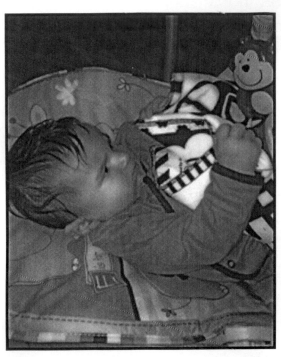

4.3. **I love handling this cloth book.**

4. Stories on television, Audio CD and DVD

Why are these important?

There are concerns about very young children watching a lot of television programmes and DVDs on the grounds that it might lead to passivity. But today's children grow up in a cultural context in which stories are experienced in different media. Reading or listening to a story read aloud from a print book and watching a film on television or a DVD are different kinds of experience. Quality children's programmes and films communicate through vision, words and sound and watched for short periods of time should be fine. The important thing is that the experience should be as interactive as possible and some suggestions follow. It is also a good idea to limit TV watching to a few set periods a day (perhaps half an hour in the morning and evening).

Interactive activities children can engage in

- Adult to point out things on the screen to discuss—What do you think might happen next? Why is that character upset?
- Join in the narration of the tale (if they already know it from the print version or from multiple viewings)
- Retell the story with the sharing adult and talk about it

- Retell the story using some props—you can improvise from your soft toy or finger puppet collection
- Make a collage picture of some of the characters. For example, children love sticking on bits of wool to create a Gruffalo creature
- Drama and role play with adult taking some of the parts

Some favourite programmes

The Gruffalo based on the story by Julia Donaldson and Axel Scheffler. ASIN BOO2UOZYG. Colour PAL (U).

This is a story about a little mouse who journeys through the wood to find a nut. On his way he meets predatory animals: a fox, an owl and a snake. The mouse thinks of an ingenious way of avoiding being eaten by the animals he meets: he invents a creature and calls it a Gruffalo. The film stays true to the illustrations and story structure in the print book on which it is based. Experiencing this film version of the tale with the sound effects, music and animation is different from listening to the book read aloud. The film version also differs in using the rather charming device of a mother squirrel telling the story to her squirrel kittens.

Tellytubbies: Time for Teletubbies, ASIN:BOO1DKoFHO, Studio; 2 Entertain Video; *Teletubbies: Musical Rhyme Time.* Studio: 2 Entertain Video. ASIN: BOO15083LW.

Available on TV and in DVD format, these stories continue to absorb the attention of younger pre-school children. Children are unlikely to remain passive once they hear the music and start to dance, jump, laugh and play alongside the teletubbies. Sometimes criticised for lack of conventional language input, children are introduced in meaningful contexts to concepts like open and shut, soft and loud, inside and outside and so on.

In the Night Garden: ASIN: BOOIEHF27E

Right from the beginning of the DVD when the adult makes the circle on the child's hand before being transported to the magical night garden, participation is encouraged. With a light touch, children are introduced to concepts of number, colour and shape. There are tactile print versions of the stories and we find children enjoy the stories in both media. The print versions give scope for talk about the characters and what they do.

Thomas the Tank Engine: Thomas and Friends. Studio: Hit. ASIN:BOO37TVOEW.

Based on the books by the Rev. W, Awdry, the film version has a catchy tune and lots of movement. Like the print versions, the film teaches about moral and practical dilemmas through the adventures of some endearing little characters that happen to be railway engines and comes out on the side of fair play. The colour, movement and the mobile faces of the engines all add to the enjoyment of this multimedia version of the superb stories. Watching the films can lead to talk, art work and savouring of the print versions of the stories.

Pingu Series 1w: Studion: Hit. ASIN:BOO3M8ZGIA.

This film about a family of penguins in their icy environment is full of visual humour. There are lots of Pingu books and the soft toys can be used to act out some of the scenes with adult input. The films and books encourage laughter, talk and role play.

Pop go the Wiggles! Nursery Rhymes and Songs. www.thewiggles.com, Studio: Hit entertainment. ASIN:BOO1E8V6EQ.

Interaction is built into this lively presentation of traditional nursery rhymes. The young Australian team use dance, improvisation, costume and props imaginatively so that Jack and Jill, Pussycat, Pussycat, Mary, Mary and many other rhymes benefit from a very lively presentation. Children love joining in with the singing and dancing and can try out using some bits of costume and props in their own renditions later on.

Audio CDs

Books and materials for children reflect the highly visual world we live in. However, if given encouragement, children from about 14 months enjoy listening to music and to stories on CDs. Car journeys can be made more interesting and children are often keen to listen to their favourites again and again. The music and sound effects should enhance the story.

Favourites include:

The Gruffalo written by Julia Donaldson and illustrated by Axel Scheffler, read by Imelda Staunton, Nacmillan Digital Audio, ISBN 978-1-4050-0518-0

The Very Hungry Caterpillar and Other Stories with audio CD. Harper Collins, reader Juliet Stevenson.

The Tiger That Came to Tea Audion CD. Harper Collins, reader Geraldine McEwan.

Timmy time Created by Jackie Cockle, written by Wayne Jackman, read by Josie Lawrence. Aardman ISBN 978-186022499-7

These four short stories about a little lamb and his friends at Nursery are beautifully read by Josie Lawrence and enhanced by jolly songs and sound effects.

The Wheels on the Bus. ISBN 978 1408 427569. AudioGO Ltd. 2010

4.4a. I'm playing with my big brothers' DVDs

4.4 b. Lots to see and talk about while we look at our i-pad.

4.4 c. It's my turn to have the i-pad!

. Information stories: stories to encourage talk about everyday experiences

Why are these important?

These stories, often termed 'information stories' stay close to real experience—starting school, going on a nature walk or visiting the dentist—and the narrative form is a vehicle for learning about the real world. They appeal to pre-school children who like to have their own experiences reflected back.

Interactive activities children can engage in

- Learn and talk about elements of the book. For example, Eric Carle's 'The very Busy Spider' calls out for explaining how a spider builds her web. The book is touchable and so children can feel the strands as well as look at the pictures
- Make the noises of animals, vehicles etc in the book and point to interesting elements e.g. bodily features like eyes, feet and tails
- Enjoy the visual details, for example, in 'The very Busy Spider' children like searching for the fly which is on every page until it is finally caught in the web

- Savour what they have seen during a nature w
  or enjoy hearing the book read aloud before th
  go outside (for example looking for spiders c
  trucks or red cars)
- Make a collage picture inspired by a particular
  book. For example reading 'The very Busy Spider'
  could lead to creating a spider using crayons or
  paints and gluing on bits of paper or material to
  make the legs

The Very Busy Spider by Eric Carle, Puffin.

This informational narrative tells of a spider's day as she gradually, and with great concentration, builds her web. Multi-sensory, it is visually alive with superb pictures of the farm animals, tactile and has a minimalist but lively written text.

Eddie's Garden by Sarah Garland, Frances Lincoln.

'Can I have a garden of my own?' asked Eddie. The family go to the garden shop and bring back seeds to plant. Detailed advice about how to grow Eddie's plants—including carrots, lettuce and sunflowers—is given as well as some safety notes. This is an ideal story to read to children before, during or after they try some planting of their own. Age 2+

...ch by Pat Hutchins, Red Fox

...he 'Titch' books, first published in the 1970s, remain favourites because they show what it is like to be the youngest in a family. You tend to get handed down clothes, the smallest bike and less grown-up presents. The text and pictures are an excellent starting point for talk, comments and questions. Age 2+

Maisy's Train by Lucy Cousins, Walker

This sturdy board book, die-cut into the shape of a little green train, has appeal even for children only about six months old. It is a wonderful introduction to transport and journeys and, as it travels through tunnels and valleys, children can join in with 'toot, toot!' and 'wheee . . .' Soon they will be saying 'Hello' to the geese, birds and butterflies as the train trundles past.

Going to the Dentist by Anne Civardi and Stephen Cartwright (illustrator), Usborne

One of the First Experiences titles (others include *Moving House* and *Going to a Party*) this one tells of a brother and sister's trip to the dentist. The waiting room and dentist's chair are pictured and there is advice from the dentist about caring for teeth. There are stickers to place in the text and children enjoy spotting the yellow duck on each page. The book is a good starting point for shopping for toothbrushes and toothpaste and setting up a good dental routine. From age 2+

A Ruined House by Mick Manning, Walker Books

Too advanced for the under fives? I find even under threes love listening to the story of the old house that has not been lived in for a long time. The pictures of owls, mice, beetles, lichen and nettles show the kind of detail children love: the pattern on feathers, the distinctive faces of the owls and the delicate marks on the wings of insects. The book suggests what young explorers can look for and it's a powerful starting point for a child's questions and observations.

Early fact books: concept books and alphabets

Why are these important?

Concept books including those on number, opposites, shapes, colour and comparisons help children categorise aspects of their world and encourage observation leading to thinking, questions and comments. Alphabet books help develop an interest in letters and words. The best early fact books are visually alive and use humour and may have special devices like pop-ups to draw young listeners in. At the pre-school stage the emphasis should be on fun, but there are some activities worth trying for children approaching three.

Charlie and Lola Shapes by Lauren Child, Orchard Books.

'I know all my shapes . . . And some EXTREMELY unusualish ones'. This concept book (like Lauren Child's other books on subjects like opposites and colours) is full of humour and quirky asides. Shapes in the everyday environment are shown—for example the crescent moon and the banana Lola holds are examples of curved shapes.

Children can:

- Talk about the shapes on each page and wh Charlie and Lola are doing
- Talk about the shapes in the room where they are listening to the book read aloud using words like 'curved', 'straight', 'angled', 'pointy' and 'even'. (For help in recognising and drawing a star—track down Eric Carle's delightful *Draw me a Star*, Puffin).
- Children approaching age three may like sorting some shapes into groups or drawing some favourite shapes, for example round shapes such as the moon, a balloon, the sun and a ball. This helps them learn about how we categorise this aspect of the world.

Other favourite concept books and alphabets include: *Farm 123* by Rod Campbell, Campbell Books. Numbers are linked to exciting happenings during a day on the farm in this beautifully illustrated lift-the-flap book which is perfectly designed for the pre-school age group. We have a large farm cat representing number one, and later, a group of mischievous rabbits show children what ten looks like. There is lots to talk about and laugh at here.

Yuck! by Mick Manning and Brita Granstrom, Frances Lincoln.

All sorts of babies eat their favourite food—rotten eggs, spiders and other unpalatable things. But unpalatable to

...m? The book has superb and amusing illustrations
...a the rhythmic text encourages the enjoyment of
...outing 'Yuck! as each baby's food is shown. Children
talk about what different animals eat and what a human
baby likes. 18 months +

That's not My Puppy Fiona Watts, Usborne

Like the others in this very successful 'That's not my . . .'
series this book helps children from about 18 months
compare and contrast. Sharing the book allows children
to join in with the text and reinforces the concept of
comparison.

Most Amazing Hide-and-Seek Alphabet Book by Robert
Crowther, Walker

A masterpiece of paper engineering with its ingenious
tabs and flaps, this book makes the alphabet dynamic
as birds pop put and creatures twist and wriggle. It
is sophisticated and needs to be enjoyed with close
supervision. If you prefer something exciting but a
little less elaborate, try *Robert Crowther's Surprise abc*
(Walker) or one of the many hundreds of abcs on the
market. Choose one that is likely to intrigue and enthuse
for 4+.

Pepper Pig's abc, Ladybird.

A good value alphabet book which provides an interactive way to learn your abc. As children approach age 2 they will enjoy using the stickers.

'Books can be read to children at anytime, but we have a routine of bedtime reading and sharing—favourites at the moment are a story about rabbits and a fact book about dinosaurs'. Father of 3.

4.6a. Front cover of *Yuck!* By Mick Manning and Brita Granstrom. Reproduced with the permission of the publishers, Frances Lincoln Ltd. Copyright 2005.

Fact books as children get older

Some children are able to appreciate more advanced books than their age would suggest as they reach three or fours years. This is more likely to be the case when the child has developed a strong interest in a topic and where an adult takes time to look at the book with them, and perhaps read it out loud and answer questions. Topics like dinosaurs, and whales, knights and castles, journeys and transport and mammals and mini beasts seem to be amongst those that appeal. Important things to look for when choosing books to inspire are good illustrations and a lively written text and an author who has the ability to communicate their enthusiasm for the topic. A speculative approach and a willingness to point out what is not yet known helps too. Children often love to choose which is their favourite theory of why the dinosaurs became extinct. Yes—it is this questioning, wondering approach we need to encourage! Karen Wallace's book *Think of an Eel*, a title in Walker Books 'Read and Wonder' series, has a lyrical written text, luminous illustrations and an intriguing secret to impart. Publishers who specialise in children's non-fiction include Usborne, Dorling Kindersley and Franklin Watts; Frances Lincoln and Walker Books often choose lyrical authors and illustrators for their non-fiction titles.

Visiting museums and places of interest can often spark off an interest. The 4 year old pictured below became eager to learn more about dinosaurs after visiting The Natural History Museum's dinosaur rooms. However, like adults, children enjoy different books for different reasons and at different times. The same boy who has an encyclopaedic knowledge of dinosaurs, often asks to be read to from a little lift-the-flap book about rabbits—a favourite from his babyhood. At night time these images seem comforting and reassuring perhaps.

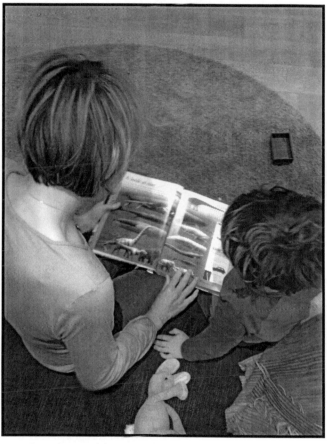

4.6 b. I love talking about my dinosaur book with Mummy.

7. Making wonder books

Before they can write, children enjoy making books with an adult's help. This helps them understand how a book works, about pages, beginnings and endings, illustrations and writing. Wonder or Interest books might arise from activities suggested in other parts of this book. For example Nature Observation Walk or In the Park or Garden, numbers 2 and 5 from Section 3 'Fun Out of Doors'. They can be about a holiday, a visit to a museum, the zoo or the park wood or pond. Or they could show all the things the child is interested in. Children love selotaping their finds to pages, too—horse chestnuts, twigs and leaves.

What you need

A sugar paper book, either bought or made out of sheets of sugar paper

Felt tipped pens or crayons

Glue or selotape

Scissors

Camera/mobile 'phone

☆ Steps

- Decide on what the book is going to be about, giving the child freedom to think about it
- Ask what they would like to go in their book
- Ask the children to stick in the pictures, photographs, drawings and, if appropriate, samples of leaves, stones and nuts.
- Let them tell you what to write, e.g. 'I found this acorn in the garden today' or 'This is a picture of the dinosaur I saw at the museum'.

Hints and tips

- Some children are more willing to do this at an early age than others—it should not be a chore
- Showing the book to Daddy or Granny or a family friend reinforces a child's feeling that it is a worthwhile activity

4.7. Illustration of Wonder Book

Postscript

Young children who explore, play, role play and hear stories and rhymes are creating a 'space' for the enjoyment of all things cultural. Donald Winnicott, the well respected child psychiatrist, calls this space 'the third area' between inner and outer experience. This 'space' needs to be nurtured in the earliest years to ensure children grow up to be creative and confident. We hope the experiences and ideas shared in this book will help.